Forew

The last fo᠎᠎᠎᠎᠎ oyne of the
WEA (Work᠎᠎᠎ ᠎ad
supported ᠎᠎᠎᠎ ᠎᠎᠎ ᠎᠎᠎᠎᠎᠎᠎ 1984 version and the 2008
edition. This third edition is a very modest update, mainly
as a result of having run out of the last lot.

I thought it was worth doing what is really little more than a re-print of the second edition because of the continuing interest in Bolton's links with Walt Whitman and the fascinating light the story shines on some neglected themes of radical politics. The sub-title of the booklet is 'spirituality, socialism and sex in a Northern mill town'. As a friend commented, there isn't much sex in it really (sorry, thought it might have helped sales) but there's quite a lot of spirituality. And perhaps that is something that has been missing from 'socialism' over the last eighty or so years. A sense of the spiritual was absolutely central to the politics of Keir Hardie, Philip Snowden, Katharine and Bruce Glasier, Caroline Martyn and so many more pioneers of early socialism. They were definitely on to something. One person who developed that integration of spirituality and socialism more than perhaps any other was J W Wallace, the fountain-head and jokingly-named 'master' of the Bolton Whitman group.

He was aided and abetted by Bolton's 'romantic radical' Allen Clarke, who played a minor role in the Whitman circle but occasionally called in to see Wallace when he was cycling between Bolton and Blackpool. You can read about Clarke, or 'Teddy Ashton', in my book *Lancashire's Romantic Radical*, which is still available.

We need to re-discover that connection of spirituality and socialism in a way that is relevant to the modern day. Maybe there's a new book project if I get time in between trains.

Paul Salveson
Slaithwaite, May 2016

CONTENTS

Front cover: Bolton's Whitman Group in its prime – Rivington, July 1894.
Back cover: The 3rd Generation – Barrow Bridge, 31 May 2001.

PREFACE TO THE 2016 EDITION

I wrote most of this book in 1984. It was published by Bolton branch of the Workers Educational Association as 'Loving Comrades – Lancashire's Links to Walt Whitman'. It deals with a small group of clerks, clergymen and skilled workers in Bolton between the 1880s and the 1920s.

I have amended the original and added a new introductory essay which was written in 2007. It has been further updated in 2016.

I owe a great debt to the staff of Bolton Public Library for the marvellous assistance they have given me – both in researching the original text in 1983/4 and in producing this new edition. Many thanks!

The original work owes much to the assistance of the staff of John Rylands Library, Manchester; Sheffield City Library; Liverpool University Library; and Bolton Evening News Library. This second edition incorporates additional information from The Library of Congess, New York Public Library, Walt Whitman Birthplace, Walt Whitman Home in Camden New Jersey, and Stanford University. My thanks to the kind and friendly assistance I received at each of these institutions. I am also indebted to the British Academy and the US Embassy for financial support in making that trip in 1985 possible.

I was privileged to have used Ruth and Eddie Frow's Working Class Movement Library in Manchester and to count both as good friends. Both Ruth and Eddie are now dead, Ruth surviving her husband by many years and passing on in January 2016. I owe both of them a huge debt of gratitude for so many things.

Bolton's Whitman links have been well and truly re-established and the work of Ed Folsom, Joann Krieg and Mike Robertson has taken studies of the Bolton – Whitman link to a much higher level. This book is an introduction to a fascinating part of Bolton's history, but also casts some interesting light on Whitman's relationship to England and the diversity and creativity of English Socialism in the late nineteenth century.

Paul Salveson

May 2016

INTRODUCTORY ESSAY
With Walt Whitman in Bolton

Walt Whitman didn't actually come to Bolton. He never left the United States, and didn't stray far from New York. Yet it feels like he came here, breathing in the Lancashire moorland air whilst striding up to Walker Fold and Rivington. To many of his friends and comrades whom he described as 'those splendid Bolton fellows', Whitman was there amongst them when they celebrated his birthday with readings, lilac and loving cups.

The great Bolton writer, Allen Clarke, said in 1919 that 'it is fitting that Bolton should be distinguished above all towns in England by having a group of Whitman enthusiasts, for many years in close touch, by letter and visit, with 'the Master', for I am sure Walt Whitman, the singer of out-door life, would have loved to ramble our Lancashire moorlands.' (published in book form in 'Moorlands and Memories', Bolton, 1920).

Why Bolton? Whitman, towards the end of his life, developed a friendship with a small group of enthusiasts in the town which was then at the heart of the Lancashire cotton industry. They called themselves 'The Eagle Street College' after the modest two-up two-down terraced house where the group's mentor, J.W. Wallace, lived with his parents in the mid-1880s. It all started with a birthday greeting sent to Whitman in1887, signed by Wallace and his friend Dr John Johnston.

The group were, at least initially, mainly lower middle-class men who included clerks, a journalist, clergymen and one or two skilled workers. They were not a metropolitan intelligentsia, but neither could they be described as representative of Bolton's industrial working class. They were probably typical of the sort of person drawn to the young Independent Labour Party with its message of ethical, rather than Marxian, socialism. As Fred Wild, an early member of the group commented *'these young men were all from the Parish Church and for the most part were engaged as clerks or minor gaffers and were attracted to Wallace by his personality and intellectual powers.'*

The story of the group casts light on the genesis of English

A Walter Crane design of the 1890's forecasting the dawn of socialism.

socialism and shows the powerful influence Whitman exerted on North of England radicalism in the early 1890s, much of which was down to the tireless proselytising of Wallace. By the beginning of the twentieth century Bolton was at the heart of an informal network of British and Irish Whitman admirers which included Keir Hardie, Robert Blatchford, Edward Carpenter, AE (George Russell) and John Addington Symonds. It extended to include some of the leading figures on the American left – including Horace Traubel, J. W. Lloyd and Leonard D. Abbott. The 'outer periphery' included railroad union leader Eugene Debs and the mother of American anarchism, Emma Goldman.

The heady mix of socialism, sexuality, mysticism and love

of 'the open air' which Carpenter personified was far from being the preserve just of well-known upper class radicals and the Bolton group took all of these themes to its heart.

Lancashire's Whitman heritage is still very much alive. 'Loving Comrades', written on an ancient Olympia typewriter back in 1984, played some part in its revival. American Whitman scholars are now regular visitors to Bolton, where the Library has one of the best Whitman archives outside the USA, which includes a very rare first edition of 'Leaves of Grass' – as well as his stuffed canary, a tea set which belonged to Whitman and a large collection of letters and photographs.

The heritage is more than a purely literary one. Each year on Whitman's birthday – May 31st or the nearest Saturday to it - members and friends of Bolton Socialist Club, a direct descendant of Bolton radicalism in the 1890s, celebrate his birthday with a walk on the moors and readings from his work. A loving cup containing spiced claret is past round and participants, wearing sprigs of lilac, take turns to read their favourite Whitman poem.

'Those splendid Bolton fellows'

Wallace, as he liked to be known, was the centre of the group. He was often called - only slightly tongue in cheek - 'The Master'. He was particularly close to his mother whose death in 1885 affected him enormously, triggering a spiritual crisis which led him to what he called a higher level of spiritual awareness.

Some members of the group took certain aspects of the Whitman 'creed' with a healthy pinch of salt whilst enjoying

Dr Maurice Bucke (centre) with Whitman group in Bolton. Wallace is to Bucke's right, August 25th 1891.
Others, l-r: Sam Hodgkinson, Thomas Shorrock, Rev. A.R.C. Hutton, Wentworth Dixon, Dr John Johnston, Fred Wild, Edward Carpenter (rear), R.K. Greenhalgh, W.A. Ferguson.

Walt Whitman in 1890 (by Dr John Johnston).

the intellectual comradeship and sense of fun which pervaded many aspects of the group's activities. Not so Wallace, who applied missionary zeal to his work and that of the group. Wallace was an enigmatic character. His public writing suggests a didactic and perhaps tedious person. However, the people who came into contact with Wallace loved him. The term 'guru' could be accurately applied to Wallace and the role he had within the group. Another early member of the group, Wentworth Dixon described him as *'the very embodiment of the perfect friend' adding 'I only wish I had the ability to portray to you the almost unique man he was – the nobility and beauty of his personality, his loving kindness, sympathy and helpfulness to everyone regardless of condition.'*

The co-founder of the group who co-signed that epochal first letter to Whitman (enclosing a cheque for £10!) was Dr John Johnston, a Bolton GP. Like Wallace he was active in the socialist movement but also played an active role in a range of local institutions, including Bolton Lads' Club, The Progressive League and medical associations. He managed to find time to be an instructor for the Lancashire and Yorkshire Railway's ambulance classes. A remarkable man who deserves a biography.

Other early members of the group included the likeable cotton waste merchant Fred Wild, who was fond of reciting humourous Lancashire dialect stories but was also a leading member of the Bolton Labour Church and Independent Labour Party. His grandson is alive and well and owns some of Fred's paintings.

Whitman sent regular messages to the Bolton group and described them as 'staunch tender fellows'. The Bolton group built up a very strong relationship with many of Whitman's American friends which continued decades after the poet's death on March 26th 1892 and is perpetuated in the strong links between Bolton and American Whitman scholars today.

An early reading group

The origins of the group lie in mid-1880s Bolton amidst the stirrings of a new politics which had a strong ethical and semi-religious slant to it. Wallace and his small group of friends saw Whitman as a prophet of the new age and met weekly in Wallace's house on Eagle Street from 1885, discussing Whitman and other poets and philosophers of the time. They were a kind of 'reading group' which has become popular once again.

The Whitman link started in earnest when the friends sent Whitman that first letter in 1887. Whitman returned their thanks and started, perhaps to his surprise as much as the Bolton group, a correspondence which ran until his death five years later. Both Wallace and Johnston visited Whitman at his home in Camden New Jersey, bringing back various trophies including a signed copy of the first edition of 'Leaves of Grass'.

Wallace in his kitchen at Babylon Lane, c.1914.

Celebrating Whitman's birthday

The highlight of the group's calendar was always Whitman's birthday, May 31st. Initially the birthday parties were held at Wallace's house in Bolton though his move to the semi-rural village of Adlington allowed the group to take advantage of the stunning moorland landscape as the location for celebrating 'the good grey poet'. Each member would wear a sprig of lilac in their lapels, and enjoy 'the gleesome saunter o'er fields and hillsides' with readings from Whitman and copious supplies of spiced claret, passed round in an ornamental loving cup brought back from one of Wallace's trips to America. And if it rained they could stay inside and have sandwiches and cakes provided by Wallace's housekeeper Minnie Whiteside.

Alice Collinge, a Bolton teacher and talented poet became involved in the group in its later years, taking time off from a demanding job and her work for the ILP and women's suffrage to attend Whitman Day and similar gatherings. Her political activities brought her into contact with Edward Carpenter, the socialist feminist Eva Gore-Booth and the Sinn Fein MP Countess Markievicz.

Visitors to Adlington included Keir Hardie, Edward Carpenter and friends from North America. These included the anarchist J.W. Lloyd who edited the 'Free Commune' and the Canadian Richard Maurice Bucke, manager of the Ontario Lunatic Asylum and originator of the term 'cosmic consciousness'.

Mysticism and sexuality on the moors

The influence of Edward Carpenter, one of the leading figures in English Socialism before the First World war and sadly neglected today, became very strong by the mid-1890s. Some of the Bolton group, particularly Charles Sixsmith, applied Carpenter's blend of sex and spirituality with gusto. He alarmed local sensibilities by making love to his wife in the back garden and also carried on a torrid affair with a young American mystic and artist called Philip Dalmas.

Much debate took place during the 1970s in US Whitman circles about the poet's sexuality, and certainly his 'Calamus' poems strongly suggest that Whitman had a sexual attraction towards men despite his own, often vehement, denials. Carpenter, who played a leading role in the emergence of modern English socialism in the 1890s, was quite overt in his own sexuality and lived with his lover, Charles Merrill, at their Sheffield farmstead for many years. Carpenter undoubtedly encouraged the Bolton group to experiment both sexually and spiritually and Johnston accompanied Carpenter on a visit to Morocco some time in the mid-1890s. They were photographed picnicking in the Moroccan countryside, Carpenter, his lover Merrill and Johnston, and an adjacent camel behind them. (See page 25).

The New Politics

Many members of the Whitman group were part of that ethical socialism movement which swept the North of England in the 1890s. The agent of this 'new religion' was the Independent Labour Party and Wallace was an active member of the Bolton branch. He used his membership to influence some of the leading figures of the ILP, including Hardie but also Robert Blatchford, editor of the mass circulation 'Clarion' newspaper, Katherine and John Bruce Glasier. Whitman's combination of democracy, love of the open air and a vague non-sectarian spirituality gave him iconic status amongst many British socialists. There is surely a book to be written on the influence of Whitman on British socialism – it was profound.

Wallace played his political cards extremely well and became an influential figure on the left of the national ILP. The Glasiers were particularly frequent visitors to Wallace's home and he and Katherine were very close.

Wallace's correspondents

Bolton Library possesses a substantial archive of letters from Wallace's wider circle of friends. Thanks to the efforts of the library's staff, these have now been properly catalogued and preserved.

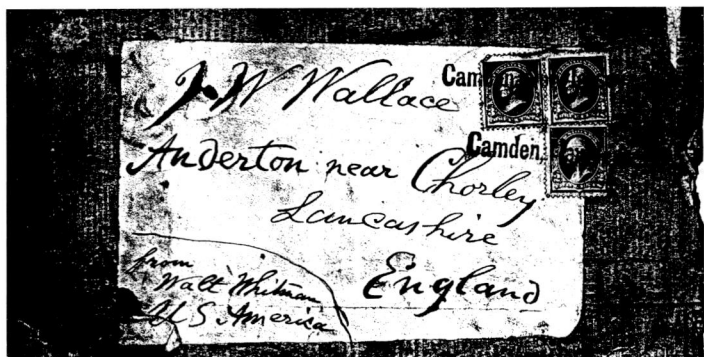

Cover of papers sent to Wallace from Walt Whitman.

The correspondence with AE, or George Russell, is particularly interesting. He was an artist, mystic and co-operator, who edited the 'Irish Homestead'. AE and Horace Plunkett established dozens of co-operative creameries across rural Ireland, showing a very practical alter ego to AE's mysticism. AE was also actively involved in Ireland's independence struggle and his correspondence with Wallace between 1919 and 1922 has numerous commentaries on the war raging across southern Ireland, with many of the new creameries being burnt out by the Black and Tans.

Keir Hardie became a close confidant of Wallace's, pouring out his feelings of isolation and disenchantment with the arid political life at Westminster.

The most extensive correspondence was with Horace Traubel, Whitman's closest companion towards the end of the poet's life. Traubel produced several volumes of conversations with his master ('With Walt Whitman in Camden') which often refer to Wallace and the Bolton group. Traubel described himself as an 'anarchist communist' and was close to the circle of American anarchists which included Max Eastman, Emma Goldman, Leonard D Abbott and J W Lloyd. Traubel edited 'The Conservator' a monthly review which combined libertarian politics with Whitmanite musings. It was financed by Joseph Fels, the Philadelphia soap millionaire and left-wing benefactor. Traubel died in 1936 but his widow Anne continued corresponding with Minnie Whiteside for many years after.

The group matures

The exclusively male character of the group changed after the First World War. Several women became active participants in the group, including the poet Alice Collinge. By the late 1920s Minnie Whiteside, initially Wallace's housekeeper, had became not only his adopted daughter but an equal participant in the group.

Other members included ILP activists and Unitarians. A later recruit to the group was John Ormrod who was very much a part of Bolton's cotton bourgeoisie. He was the first man in Bolton to own a car and lived in a stylish, though not palatial house at Walker Fold, on the Bolton moors. From the mid-1920s the annual gatherings nearly always took place at Ormrod's.

Death and re-birth

Following Wallace's death in 1926, Minnie Whiteside acted as unofficial organiser of the group and continued the birthday parties and periodic gatherings. She married, becoming Mrs Bull, and moved to a semi in Bolton's suburbs. She maintained contact with many of the American Whitman scholars including Verne Dyson, Will S.

A delightful picture of the group in Wallace's backyard, Babylon Lane c.1910. Johnston, Wallace and Wentworth Dixon at front – Minnie Whiteside looking slightly bored in the background. Nightingale and Wild behind with unknown visitor to their right.

Back row l-r: Sixsmith, Law, Wentworth Dixon, unknown, Wild. Front row: Greenhalgh, Wallace, Johnston.

Monroe and Charles E. Feinberg. Anne Traubel wrote to her in 1946 about her feelings for Wallace, who had been dead some 20 years: *'Minnie – I dare not dare speak of the feeling that accompanies my daily thoughts and memories. Our friend who filled the earth and sky with benefaction'.*

By the mid 1950s the meetings had died out. The 'Second Generation' of Bolton Whitmanites was at an end.

1984 Revival

The revival of the Bolton Whitman connection took place in the mid-1980s. Members of the Bolton Socialist Club, whose history goes back to 1888 and the early days of Bolton Whitmania, discovered the Whitman connection through a revived interest in the local writer and socialist Allen Clarke, who was a friend of Dr Johnston's. An account in Clarke's 'Moorlands and Memories' of the 'Whitman Day' celebration in 1913 led to my spending many long and fascinated hours going through the Whitman archives in Bolton Library. The first revived 'Whitman Day' took place in 1984 and co-incided with publication of 'Loving Comrades'. This was followed by a trip to the United States to look through Whitman archives in New York, Washington, Philadelphia and California. This is described in more detail in Chapter 10. In many ways the visit itself was more important than the research, helping to re-establish strong links with the American Whitman community. These have continued and strengthened. This year, 2008, sees the 25th anniversary of the revived Whitman Day celebration.

The significance of the Bolton group

On one level, the story of the Bolton Whitmanites is a charming and quirky tale of little more than local significance. But there is more to it. US Whitman scholars have long recognized the significance of Whitman's links to Bolton and the importance with which he treated those 'splendid Bolton fellows'. The archive material in Bolton Library now sees regular use by both American and British academics.

Much writing on the development of British socialism tends to stress the influence of William Morris and John Ruskin. The role of Edward Carpenter has been seriously under-played and one wonders if this was partly because of Carpenter's sexuality and mysticism becoming an embarrassment to the more conventional leaders of the Labour Party in the twentieth century.

Carpenter was heavily influenced by Whitman and his writings and speeches are drenched with Whitman references. The Bolton group, in turn, influenced, and were influenced by, Carpenter. What Wallace in particular achieved was getting Whitman placed centre-stage in the pantheon of socialist 'heroes'. He achieved this through skilful lobbying of people like Hardie, Blatchford and the Glasiers. Whitman's message struck a strong chord with Keir Hardie's emotional socialism. Whitman's celebration of nature and the 'open air' chimed with the early socialist movement's emphasis on walking and cycling. The Clarion Cycling Club, inspired by Blatchford's 'Clarion' newspaper, was probably the most successful example of the left's attempts to provide a 'social' side to its activities, at least in the UK.

This lively, open-minded and slightly eccentric political culture which emerged in the 1890s did not endure. The tragedy of British Socialism is the tragedy of the European Left, with many of its finest activists dragged into the First World War. The world that emerged after 1918 was less hospitable to the ethical, sexual and spiritual messages that Whitman and his disciples espoused.

Whitman's last letter to Wallace and Johnston was dated February 7th, some six weeks before he died:

'...More and more it comes to the fore that the only theory worthy of our modern times for great literature politics and sociology must combine all the bulk-people of all lands, the women not forgetting. But the mustard plaster on my side is singing and I must stop – Good-bye to all.'

The———

PROGRESSIVE LEAGUE,

and the Bolton Housing and Town Planning Association.

Monday Evening, October 21st

At 7-30 in the

NEW SPINNERS' HALL,

St. George's Road,

A LECTURE

Edward Carpenter, M.A.

Author of "Towards Democracy."

SUBJECT:

" BEAUTY IN CIVIC LIFE."

Dr. J. JOHNSTON, of Lostock, will Preside.

Admission Free. Retiring Collection.
Tickets for Reserved Seats, One Shilling each.

From Mr. W. M. Farrington, or Mr. J. Darbyshire, 7 Corporation Chambers, Corporation Street, or at the door.

GEO. S. IKIN, Typ., Fold St., Bolton.

Carpenter speaks in Bolton on 'Beauty in Civic Life', c. 1914. Dr Johnston presided.

1. THE FLOWERING OF ENGLISH SOCIALISM

When I wrote the original introduction to 'Loving Comrades' in 1984 I said that "Socialism in Britain has been on the retreat in the last ten years; apart from the Labour Party's election setbacks, the very ideas of socialism have been under attack by the revival of a right wing ideology under Margaret Thatcher's rule. This has led to a questioning about the meaning of socialism, and how we achieve it.

The old truisms of the Left, have been challenged by the rise of new forces: such as feminism and the 'greens'. Perhaps the biggest challenge to old orthodoxies has been the recognition of the importance of personal relations: how we live our lives, sexual relations, love and our relationship to our environment. Perhaps those socialist pioneers have a stronger message to us in 2008 than they did in 1984.

The early days of the socialist movement saw an immensely rich flowering of ideas and activities. The socialist clubs and socialist Sunday schools, Clarion cycling and rambling clubs, vocal unions and debating societies suggest a socialist culture in the 1880s and '90s of great depth.

The early socialist organisations – the Social Democratic Federation, the Independent Labour Party and the myriad local groups including anarchists worked together for a common cause, at least at a local level. William Morris, Tolstoy, Kropotkin and Carpenter were as popular as the more commonly remembered figures like Keir Hardie, Marx and Engels. How much of that libertarian socialist tradition we have lost! Yet perhaps their ideas are alive in the modern green movements which have strong echoes of classic libertarian socialism.

Visit of American anarchist JW Lloyd to Rivington, 1913. Allen Clarke at the back with Wentworth Dixon to his right and Fred Wild to his left. JW Lloyd in front with hat and light coat, with Wallace and Minnie Whiteside to his left and Dr Johnston to his right, alongside Revd. Thompson.

Women played a major part in this socialist culture: Katherine Conway (later Glasier), Caroline Martyn, Enid Stacy, and Margaret Macmillan were four of the most popular socialist speakers in the early '90s, and many women were active – not always in a subordinate role – at grass roots level.

These early socialists questioned every aspect of life. The capitalist economic system was rotten certainly, and so too its liberal – tory politics. But for many socialists this criticism went further. Capitalist morality itself was obnoxious – the dual standards of Victorian morality in its oppression of women and ready use of child labour, and its religious hypocrisy.

The socialist response was as broad as its attack on capitalism: people were desperate for alternatives. Some tried communal living – such as the Daisy Colony at Blackpool, started by a group of working class socialists in Bolton who included Allen Clarke (see below). Many built up an alternative lifestyle within the thriving socialist culture of the day by being active in its club life and other social activities alongside the straight 'political' work. Some dabbled in forms of mysticism – spiritualism, faith healing and eastern religion. Herbalism, vegetarianism and 'rational dress' figured strongly in the culture.

In Bolton, every aspect of this socialist culture was reflected. If we take 1896 as an example, we find an active branch of the Social Democratic Federation, led by the popular shoemaker, Joseph Shufflebotham. Bolton Labour Church was one of the country's biggest, with the venerable old radical James Sims as president. It had close links with both the SDF and the Independent Labour Party, which had opened its new premises on Bowker's Row three years before. A section of the Clarion Cycling Club had recently been formed in the town and the socialist dialect writer Allen Clarke had just started his "Teddy Ashton's Journal". There was a strong current of liberal radicalism in the town, spearheaded by Solomon Partington, and a growing feminist movement which owed much to the work of Sarah Reddish, who later became president of the Women's Co-operative Guild.

This great depth to Bolton's socialism was not unique in Lancashire. What is distinctive in Bolton's socialist history is the connection to the great American poet of democracy, Walt Whitman. Whitman was regarded at the time as a centrally important 'prophet' of the new religion of socialism. The Whitman group in Bolton built up a network of international contacts based around a shared love of Whitman's poetry and philosophy. In Britain, it included Keir Hardie, Edward Carpenter, Katherine Conway and her future husband John Bruce Glasier. In America it included Whitman himself and socialist writers such as Horace Traubel, John Burroughs and Dr. R.M. Bucke. George Russell (AE) was a close friend in Ireland, John Addington Symonds in his Swiss retreat, and there were other friends in Canada, France and Japan.

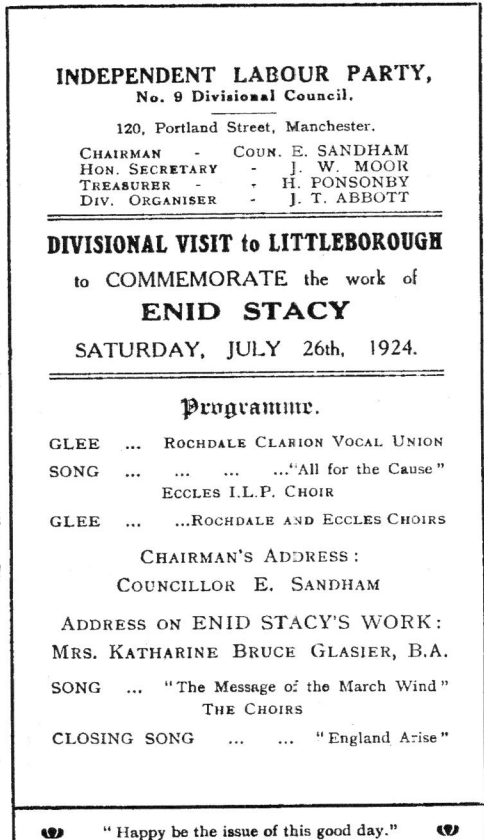

Enid Stacy was a leading ILP speaker. This commemorative event featured the Clarion Vocal Union and ILP Choir, and ended with Carpenter's 'England Arise'. Katherine Glasier was the main speaker.

The small group of clerks, clergymen and skilled workers that made up the Bolton 'Whitmanites' were a remarkable bunch. Their connection with the above 'great names' is only part of their fascination and importance. Equally interesting is the depth anc continuity of their love for each other: in many cases spanning lifetimes, and going into second and even third generations. Their capacity to discuss taboo subjects such as homosexuality casts a further interesting light on 'personal politics' in late Victorian Britain. What really bound the group together was their sense of 'loving comradeship' which they saw as a vital preliminary and essential ingredient for any socialist society worthy of the name.

Respectable revolutionaries: cn the steps of Bank Street Chapel, Bolton 1919. l-r Thompson, Johnston, Atkinson, Nightingale, Wallace, Wentworth Dixon, Broadhurst, Fred Wild. Another delayed shutter release photograph by Dr Johnston.

2. THE IMPORTANCE OF WHITMAN

Walt Whitman was the greatest American poet of the 19th century. He was born on Long Island in 1819 and died in Camden, New Jersey in 1892. During his life he was regarded as something of an eccentric figure. To the literary establishments of America and England he was an embarrassment – his poems didn't rhyme, in fact they seemed more like a shopping list than 'poetry'. He was of the common people – a printer by trade. The subject matter of his poetry was equally distasteful. If people had sex at all, it was kept out of poetry books; and to suggest that men might have more than an aloof companionship with each other was unimaginable.

Whitman didn't make a lot of money writing his poetry. A few recognised him as a truly revolutionary poet whose greatness would outlast his critics – Emerson being one of the first to give Whitman the recognition he deserved. Later, he was given immense support by a small group of intellectuals including Horace Traubel, John Burroughs, Dr. R. M. Bucke, Herbert and Anne Gilchrist.

In England, W. Rossetti was the first to publicise the new radical poetry of Whitman; John Addington Symonds and Edward Carpenter – both gay intellectuals but separated politically and in their attitude to women – did much to get Whitman known in English literary circles. Carpenter went beyond this small circle, and began to get Whitman known in the labour movement. He visited the poet in 1877 and again seven years later. He saw him as a prophetic figure. Carpenter's poems in "Towards Democracy" were consciously based on Whitman's work and helped increase Whitman's own popularity, particularly in the British socialist movement.

What was it that so endeared Whitman to socialists of the day? Carpenter suggests the central reason being his capacity for love...........

"He was a man in whom the power of love was developed to an extraordinary degree. Yet (thanks to him) this was no attenuated or merely spiritual love, but was a large and generous passion, spiritual and emotional of course, but well rooted in the physical and sexual also. In him the various sides and manifestations of the passions were so blended that instead of weakening they recognised and reinforced each other.........piercing through the layers of caste, through differences of race, climate, character and occupation; despising distances of space and time; he drew men and women of the most varied nature and habits to himself..... "Leaves of Grass" is the meeting ground of the human race. There every nationality, every creed, every trade, every atom of humanity is represented, and all are fused in the great loving soul that overbroods them."

(Edward Carpenter "Days with Walt Whitman")

Whitman's love poetry is remarkably fresh – even startling in some respects. His sexuality remains a puzzle to this day: there can be little denying the strength of his homosexual feelings, given poetic expression in the "Calamus" poems in "Leaves of Grass", though in a rather tongue-in-cheek letter to John Addington Symonds Whitman denies any suggestions of a 'homo-erotic' motif and claims the paternity of six children! In the third "Calamus" poem Whitman describes his feelings whilst waiting for his lover, and his arrival:

"And that night, while all was still, I heard the
waters roll slowly continually up the shores,
I heard the hissing rustle of the liquid and sands,
as directed to me, whispering, to congratulate me, -
For the friend I love lay sleeping by my side,
In the stillness his face was inclined towards me,
while the moon's clear beams shone,
And his arm lay lightly over my breast –
And that night I was happy."

As well as a specific love, Whitman is writing of a much broader love of all humanity, as Carpenter demonstrates – through his poems he is attempting to establish 'the dear love of comrades' on this earth. The appeal can only be universal:

"Camerado, I give you my hand!
I give you my love more precious than money,
I give you myself before preaching and law,
Will you give me yourself? Will you come travel with me?
Shall we stick by each other as long as we live?"

To this consuming idea of love was added democracy – the celebration of the American working man and woman, the typical common pioneers that Whitman loved:

"A song for occupations!
In the labour of engines and trades and the labour
of fields I find the developments
And find the eternal meanings.
Workmen and workwomen!
Were all educations practical and ornamental well
display'd out of me, what would it amount to?
Were I as the head teacher, charitable proprietor,
wise statesman, what would it amount to?
Were I to you as the boss employing and paying you,
would that satisfy you?
The learn'd, virtuous, benevolent and the usual terms,
A man like me and never the usual terms.
Neither a servant nor a master I,
I take no sooner a large price than a small price,
I will have my own whoever enjoys me,
I will be even with you and you shall be even with me.
(from 'A Song for Occupations")

To love and democracy, a celebration of nature is Whitman's third central theme which explains his attraction to the British socialists. Socialism was very much an open-air movement in the 1890s, with rallies on the moors, rambling and botanical clubs linked in with socialist activity. The rambling notes of Allen Clarke's "Teddy Ashton's Journal" began with Whitman's clarion call: 'Whoever you are – come with me!" and it isn't difficult to recognise the appeal of a poem like "By Broad Potomac's Shore" and the lines :

"Again old heart so gay, again to you, your sense,
the full flush spring returning,
Again the freshness and the odours, again Virginia's
summer sky, pellucid blue and silver,
Again the forenoon purple of the hills,
Again the deathless grass, so noiseless, soft and green,
Again the blood red roses blooming."

Whitman never won the recognition he sought from the American workers – but the extent to which he captured the hearts of British working class socialists is remarkable. The appeal founded on love and comradeship, democracy and nature was irresistible to the strongly ethical-based socialism of the north. Robert Blatchford, editor of the "Clarion", did more than anyone to express that sort of socialism in a popular way, and in this extract there can be no doubting his debt to Whitman, taken from "The New Religion of the North":

"This new religion which is rousing and revivifying the
north of England is something much higher and greater
than a wages question, an hours question, a franchise
question, based though it is on some of those
things..........It is a religion of manhood and womanhood,
of sweetness and of light.......for this we are indebted to
the idol-breaking of Carlyle, the ideal-making of Ruskin
and to the trumpet-tongued proclamation by the titanic
Whitman of the great message of true democracy and the
brave and sweet comradeship of the natural life – of the
stainless, virile, thorough human life, lived out boldly and
frankly in the open air and in the eyes of God."

Whitman's adoption by British socialism in the '80s and '90s owed a lot to Carpenter and particularly the efforts of the Bolton group. There is though, a contradiction. Whitman never described himself as a socialist – he was more the radical democrat typified by Lincoln and Emerson. In his later years though, at the prompting of his close friend (and socialist) Horace Traubel, he did go some way towards an acceptance of socialist ideas. Traubel recounts an incident where Whitman gets rattled at being described in a British journal as ' a socialist'. He ends by saying:

"Of course I'm a good deal more of a socialist than I
thought I was, maybe not technically, politically so, but
intrinsically, in my meanings."

Readers of Whitman undoubtedly interpreted his work in precisely this way and found great strength in his poetry. In socialist periodicals of the 1890s it was common to find adverts for "Leaves of Grass" and cheap editions of Whitman's work, alongside other socialist classics.

3. EAGLE STREET COLLEGE

The name was a joke. The 'college' was a self-deprecating reference to a group of men who met in the small terraced house at 14 Eagle Street, Bolton, belonging to J. W. Wallace. Wallace was the founder and inspiration of the Bolton Whitmanites and the story starts with him.

Wallace

J.W.Wallace – "Wallace" – was the central figure in the Bolton group. He was born in a small shop on Bridge Street in 1853. His father was a millwright who had moved down from Northumberland to find work in the Lancashire cotton industry; he later spent much time in Russia equipping new mills there. His mother was from Bolton and 'a kind gentle woman who suffered for many years the most agonising torture of rheumatism' according to Wallace's friend Fred Wild. Most of Wallace's early years were spent at 14 Eagle Street, off Bury Road, described by Wild as "one of the worst streets in the Haulgh".

At the age of 14 he started work at Bradshaw's – a local firm of architects (later Bradshaw and Gass, then Bradshaw, Gass and Hope, architects of Bolton's fine Civic Centre), with whom he stayed all his working life until his retirement in 1912. Wallace was not untypical of many bright working class children of his time. Through sympathetic parents and the opportunities afforded by the expansion of late-Victorian capitalism, he was able to rise into the ranks of the lower middle class, becoming an architect's assistant. He was dogged by poor health and bad eyesight, and moved into the more rural surroundings of Adlington in the early 1890s, living at 40 Babylon Lane. He was looked after by two housekeepers, the first being a Mrs Jones. The second was a widow of a friend of Wallace's, Minnie Whiteside. She was devoted to Wallace and he to her; eventually she came to be regarded as his adopted daughter.

Genesis of the Group

Wallace was an avid reader in his youth - an interest he shared with two close friends: Fred Wild, a cotton waste merchant who lived on Dorset Street and Dr. John Johnston, a general practitioner at 54 Manchester Road, who originated from Annan, Dumfrieshire. Fred Wild was a

Whitmanite greeting card, 1896, sent to Revd. Hutton with a collection of Edward Carpenter's books.

jovial personality but deeply cultivated. He was a talented painter and an authority on Shakespeare. His obituary in 1935 records:

"Certainly he was a personality with a leaning to the unorthodox in his interests and opinions. He was a keen socialist and Blatchfordite in the days when few men of his class were identified with left wing politics and was a lively member of debating clubs which flourished in those days,

and a founder of Bolton Labour Church."

(Bolton Evening News 23rd July 1935)

Johnston is an equally interesting figure, and led a remarkably active life. He played a leading role in medical and health issues in the town, particularly in the question of child labour in the mills. His book "The Wastage of Child Life" was a brilliant expose of the damage done to children in Bolton's mills. He spent a lot of his spare time as an instructor for the St John's Ambulance Brigade and railway ambulance classes in the Bolton area. In his diary for 1887 there is a poignant entry accompanying a news cutting about 'a fatal accident at Trinity Street station'. William Davies, a shunter, fell off a truck and was run over: both his legs were broken and his left foot was cut off. Johnston commented:

"The poor fellow was one of the members of my ambulance class and has left a wife and five children. Alas! Alas!"

(Johnston Diaries 1887)

Johnston was also involved in the Bolton Labour Church and strongly opposed both the Boer War and the First World War. Yet his humanity was such that he spent days and nights trying to repair the human damage done by the

carnage: first at Whalley Military Hospital and then at Townleys (now Royal Bolton Hospital) during the first World War.

There was a lighter side to his character. He was a keen cyclist and was often seen around town on a tricycle! He was also deeply involved in the cultural life of Bolton, apart from his activities in the Whitman group.

These three men – each exceptional in his own way – formed the nucleus of the Bolton Whitman group. They read, often together at Wallace's – the works of Burns, Carlyle, Tennyson, Ruskin and Emerson. They soon picked out Whitman as their favourite and started regular Monday evening meetings at which Whitman would be the main topic of conversation. Others, like Wentworth Dixon, joined and Johnston dubbed the group "The Eagle Street College"! 1885 was the year that the 'college' began meeting on this regular basis, coinciding with the death of Wallace's mother. Dixon describes the group, and I have added, where known, the occupations of members of the group:

"The death in 1885 of his mother, to whom he was strongly attached, caused him profound sorrow. At this period, the reading of Whitman's "Leaves of Grass" was a source of great spiritual comfort. He would recite to us with great feeling numerous passages from "Leaves". The meanings of some of these poems was somewhat obscure to several of us and caused animated discussions, but lucid explanations were always forthcoming from Wallace. The friends who foregathered at Eagle Street at this time were Fred Wild (cotton waste dealer), Dr Johnston, Richard Greenhalgh (bank clerk), William Law, Sam Hodgkinson (hosiery manufacturer), William Pimblett (engineering employers' federation secretary), Rev. Tyas, Rev. F.R.C. Hutton (St. George's Congregational Church),Richard Curwen, Thomas Shorrock (magistrate's clerk), William Ferguson (bank clerk), Fred Nightingale (clerk), myself (lawyer's clerk)."

(Wentworth Dixon "An Old Friend" – address to the Men's Class at Bank Street School. 7th February 1926)

This is not an exhaustive list of the early members of the group, which was more fluid than in later years. Wallace refers to 'two artisans' including George Humphries, a

Johnston in military attire with Whitman group c. 1916.
l-r: Broadhurst, Thompson, Johnston, Wild, Wallace, Wentworth Dixon, Minnie Whiteside, Nightingale.

millwright and an un-named eng ne driver, probably called Pullen. Later recruits in the 1890s include Rev. Scott of Harwood Unitarian Church and Charles F. Sixsmith, manager of Bentinck Mill, Farnworth. Walt Hawkins of Huddersfield became the group's chronicler in the early 1900s and often contributed a poem to celebrate each Whitman Day. Another fascinatirg member of the group was William Atkinson, who went to school with Wild and Wallace. He later moved to Cheshire and then to Midhurst, Sussex where he developed a horticultural business. He kept in close contact with the Bolton group and supplied bouquets of lilac for the Whitman Day celebrations. He was a close friend of the American anarchist J.W. Lloyd and also Edward Carpenter sharing interests not only in Whitman but also in eastern philosophy and the study of nature.

Visitors included such figures as W.M. Carr the architect and his colleague Charles Holden and L' Hoondi Raj Thangi who lived in Bolton for a few years and later became president of the Indian Congress. Fred Wild, in his genial, blunt way, describes the Bolton group:

" These young men were all from the Parish Church and for the most part were engaged as clerks or minor gaffers and were attracted to Wallace by his personality and intellectual powers, but not one of them except Dr. Johnston and myself could be called 'Whitmanites' "

(Fred Wild "Sketch of Life of J.W.Wallace of Bolton)

As Dixon honestly admitted, some of the discussion at Eagle Street tended towards the esoteric, but what does stand out is the basic continuity of the group over a very long time: Wallace, Johnston, Wild, Dixon, Ferguson, Nightingale, Shorrock and Greenhalgh remained part of the group until their deaths. What held it together? Wallace himself suggests the reason:

"Its basic element was friendship – hearty, full-blooded, intimate, free, of long growth and freighted with old associations. Another element, not less vital, was the almost religious character of our meetings which developed as time went on…………….we were old friends who could talk together on any subject quite frankly without fear of giving offence…….there were times when it led us to a deepened intimacy, in which the inmost quests of the soul were freely expressed, and each grew conscious of our essential unity, as of a larger self which included us all."

(J.Johnston and J.W.Wallace "Visits to Walt Whitman 1890-91")

Wallace's writing at this time is drenched with mystical references and symbolism, and certainly there was plenty of that in Whitman himself. However, the death of Wallace's mother does seem to have resulted in a profound change in his consciousness, what he calls an 'illumination' or entering into 'cosmic consciousness'. He later related his experiences to his Canadian Whitmanite friend Dr. R.M. Bucke, whose book "Cosmic Consciousness" was inspired by a visit to the Bolton group. Bucke placed Wallace in the category of ' lesser, imperfect and doubtful' instances of cosmic consciousness, an honour he shared with Moses, Isaiah, Socrates and Swedenborg. Wallace later linked his illumination to religious experience:

"By religious experience I mean that opening of the spiritual senses, and consequent recognition of spiritual realities as of supreme and transcendent importance, and of one's unity with the race, which when it happens to a man, so completely revolutionises his whole outlook on life and all his desires and aims as to amount to a new birth. It is the appearance within himself of a new centre of consciousness dominating all the rest, and gradually bringing them into ever closer harmony with itself."

(J.W.Wallace "Walt Whitman and Religion" lecture delivered to Progressive League, Bolton 28th March 1915)

Fred Wild also noted the effect of Wallace's illumination following his mother's death – and inward change, 'a steady calmness and air of peace' coming over him. These experiences led Wallace into a deeper study of eastern religion, sharing with Whitman and Edward Carpenter a familiarity with The Upanishads and the Bhagavad Gita.

Debates within the Group

Wallace's statement that the group could discuss any subject 'freely and frankly' was slightly disingenuous. There seem to have been very strong disagreements in the group over socialism, which led to a few of the peripheral members leaving. The three main figures in the group were, by the 1890s, active socialists. So too was Wentworth Dixon, who was involved in Bolton's Labour Church which had been formed in 1892 at the Duke's Alley Congregational Church. This irritated Tories in the group like R.K. Greenhalgh and liberals like Ferguson. Wallace wrote a long letter to the group on the 6th January 1893 in which he touched on the controversial issue:

"I am very well aware that our discussions of 'socialism' have been distasteful to some of our members who are rather hanging back in doubt as to where we are going to, and what they are likely to be committed to – and it is also felt that a series of debates on economic questions...............are not so helpful to individual members as some of our meetings in the past have been, in so far as they resulted in increased faith in the unseen and in contented acceptance of cheer."

Wallace calls for an open expression of differences which will, in the event, strengthen rather than weaken the group, bound together by comradeship and love :

"I wish for our college to stand for a higher ideal (than socialism, individualism etc), for aspiration towards a more useful and developed manhood, hospitable to ideas and to persons, warmly aiding the right and forever presenting comradeship and affection to each other."

Wallace adds that in his belief, democracy (the working class) was making rapid strides to power – 'as inevitable as gravitation' – but gives a word of warning:

"Unless the democracy is wise and religious there must necessarily be many evils resulting from its too early arrival at supreme power.

We are charged by profoundest and divine call of selection to minimise these dangers and to see to it that the greatest birth of time is indeed beneficent. For we are the heaven-appointed preachers to the democracy of England!

We stand in closest relation to Walt Whitman – the divinely inspired prophet of world democracy.

To us the leaders of English democracy will look more and more for spiritual sustenance."

The context of this letter was that socialism was making big steps forward and anyone at the time could be forgiven for thinking that a socialist government would soon be formed. However, unless the movement was underpinned by the Whitman values of love, comradeship and non-violence, the result could be as was later experienced in Russia and elsewhere. Wallace saw his role and that of the group, to spread the Whitman message throughout the socialist movement, particularly through its most influential leaders. Bolton was to be the ethical heart of British socialism.

Whitman Day 1899, at Dr Johnston's, 54 Manchester Road, Bolton.
l-r: Wentworth Dixon, Sixsmith, Wild, Greenhalgh, Wallace, Johnston.

4. WHITMAN DAY

When Wallace moved to Adlington in the early 1890s, the regular Monday evening sessions came to an end, though the group still met regularly at the houses of Wild, Johnston, Dixon or Hodgkinson. The group often went to Adlington to see Wallace and the move left the group intact.

The biggest day in the Bolton Whitmanites calendar was the anniversary of the poet's birth - 31st May. The first celebrations took place in 1885 with a small gathering at Wallace's. Birthday greetings were sent to Whitman, extracts from his work were read and a tea party followed. The occasion became more elaborate as the years went on – the celebrations being held in the open air of friends' gardens. In the 1890s, Fred Wild, Dr. Johnston and Richard Greenhalgh were frequent hosts with their gardens decorated with Whitmanesque lilac blossoms (Whitman's favourite flower – cf 'When Lilacs Last in the Dooryard Bloom'd' etc). Later, the celebrations were held at Rivington, in the garden of Rev. Thompson, the Unitarian vicar, or at the home of John Ormrod at Walker Fold. Edward Carpenter became a frequent visitor and recorded his impressions in his autobiography "My Days and Dreams":

"I have mentioned Walt Whitman more than once in the foregoing pages and I think I ought to not let this chapter pass without referring to the ardent little coterie of Bolton, Lancashire, who for many years celebrated his birthday with decorations of lilac boughs and blossoms, songs, speeches and recitations and the passing of loving cups to his memory."

Carpenter was a regular visitor to the group from 1892 onwards and other honoured guests included Keir Hardie, and Katherine and John Bruce Glasier. Alice Collinge, the Bolton poet and socialist-feminist became a member of the group through the Labour Church and recalls the Whitman Day celebration as a much needed rest from the turmoil of suffrage demonstrations and Labour Church activity:

"As a counter attraction to those hectic days, there was the restful contemplative influence of the Whitman Fellowship behind it all, and in that influence alone I owe

Wentworth Dixon

with love from

J.W. Wallace

WHITMAN DAY, 1913.

Rivington

Celebration in Bolton.

[Reprinted from *Annandale Observer* of 20th June, 1913.]

The little group of the Lancashire friends of Walt Whitman, who for twenty-eight years have met together annually to celebrate his birthday on May 31st, spent the afternoon and evening of that date this year in Rivington, a beautiful country district eight miles from Bolton, with its noted park at the base of the hill known for many miles round as "Rivington Pike."

Their host was the Rev. Samuel Thompson, minister of the quaint, old-world, Unitarian Chapel, adjoining the central "Green" of the tiny village, whose Parsonage, surrounded by tall trees, has an ideal "minister's garden" sloping down from its south front, well enclosed and protected, the unsophisticated charm of which can be nowhere surpassed. After inspecting this garden, the party wandered about the Park, visiting the ancient Barn and the Old Hall, and then returned to Mr Thompson's house for tea.

After this a short address of welcome was given by the host, and various letters were read by Dr Johnston. Several bouquets of flowers had been sent by friends at a distance, the most notable being one of forget-me-not and white lilac, sent by Mrs Hawkins in memory of her husband, who had regularly attended these anniversary meetings for several years and contributed special poems, and whose death, nearly a year ago, was very sorely felt.

an eternal debt to Bolton. To hear the late J.W.Wallace read a paper on Whitman in a Whitman atmosphere, either at Rivington, Walker Fold or the Haulgh, was a perfect inspiration and one of those special privileges one cannot account for."

(Alice Collinge : Autobiographical Notes in Bolton Library)

Messages from absent friends were read – from American friends like Traubel and Bucke, Whitman scholars like Leon Bazalgette, exiled Whitmanites such as William Atkinson of Midhurst (who supplied the lilacs) and socialists like Caroline Martyn, James Sims, Keir Hardie, Katherine Glasier and Edward Carpenter.

Wallace invariably read a prepared address on some aspect of Whitman's life and work: The "Calamus" poems, Whitman and Religion, or a particular poem. The last address he made, in 1925, had the title "If Walt Whitman Came to Walker Fold".

The loving cup Carpenter refers to was Whitman's own, and was presented to the Bolton group by J.H. Johnston of New York, in 1894. Johnston visited Bolton in June and sent the loving cup as a 'thank you' gift to the Bolton group on his return to America. American visitors to the celebration were not uncommon. In 1913, J.W. Lloyd of New Jersey was the guest. Allen Clarke describes the day, celebrating 'the great American singer of comradeship and immortality':

It was May 31st but we had rain and thunder that day – and then sunshine. But we enjoyed 'the gleesome saunter o'er fields and hillsides' and after a tour of Lever Park.......we had tea at the foot of the Pike in the old manse of the Rev. S. Thompson, our genial scotch host."

(Allen Clarke: "Moorlands and Memories")

A report of the day's events was made by Dr Johnston and published – not in a Bolton paper but the "Annandale Observer"! The doctor still had connections with his home town. Johnston was a good writer; his description of the 1913 celebration ends thus:

"As the party afterwards walked homewards through the quiet lanes and fields in the beautiful evening light, the calm atmosphere, the rich and pensive colouring of the sunset clouds, 'the slumbering and liquid trees', and the

General Idea.

5-0.	Friends to Tea.
6-0.	Greetings to Arrivals.
6-30.	Group Photograph—Mr. Broadhurst.
7-0.	Welcome—Mr. F. Wild.
7-10.	Address—Dr. J. Johnston. " Evolution of ~~Mind~~ LIFE and ~~Matter~~. CONSCIOUSNESS "

" All forces have been steadily employed
to complete and delight me—
Now on this spot I stand
with my robust soul."—W. W.

7-40.	Discussion.
8-0.	Original Poem by W. T. Hawkins.
8-30.	Address—Mr. J. W. Wallace.
8-40.	Toast to Walt and Friends.—J. W. Wallace.
8-50.	General Talk and Refreshments.
9-0.	Gramophone: Readings by " The Boys," Hawkins.
9-20.	General Talk.
10 to 11.	Au Revoir. So Long!

A printed programme for Whitman Day, at Fred Wild's, 37 Dorset Street. Expected friends included the regulars but also Joseph Fels the soap millionaire and socialist. May 31st 1907.

far-stretching landscape all seemed as if pervaded by a brooding Presence, infinitely poignant and sweet, responsive to their mood, and crowning with a fitting finale the day's celebration."

The celebration continued long after the death of both Wallace and Johnston. The people primarily responsible for this were Minnie Whiteside, William Broadhurst and John Ormrod, at whose home they were held. They lasted well into the 1950s.

5. VISITS TO WHITMAN

The visits of Dr Johnston and Wallace to Whitman are well documented, though not well known outside Whitman scholarship. The extensive correspondence between the Bolton group and Whitman began in 1887, with a birthday message and a gift of money. The first visit took place during July and August of 1890, by Dr. Johnston. He kept a detailed record of the conversations and records Whitman's greeting:

That must be a very nice little circle of friends you have at Bolton.............I hope you will tell them how deeply sensible I am to their appreciation and regard for me; and I should like you to tell all my friends in England whom you come across how grateful I am, not only for their appreciation, but for their more substantial tokens of goodwill."

(J.Johnston and J.W. Wallace "Visits to Walt Whitman")

Johnston met Whitman several times during his stay and visited numerous Whitman 'shrines' such as his birthplace at West Hills. He also met close friends of Whitman like Herbert Gilchrist and Andrew Rome. The experience was a memorable one for the doctor and his visit led to long-lasting links with American Whitman devotees.

The occasion of the second visit began with the arrival of Whitman's close friend and biographer, Dr. R.M. Bucke to visit Johnston for a few days in July 1891. He brought a message from Whitman for the Bolton group:

"What staunch tender fellows these Englishmen are! I doubt if a fellow ever had such splendid emotional send-back response as I have had from these Lancashire chaps under the lead of Dr. J. and J.W.W. – it cheers and nourishes my very heart. If you go down to Bolton, and convenient, read publicly to them the last five or six lines as if from my living pulse."

Bucke strongly urged Wallace to return to America with him – as Horace Traubel, Whitman's close friend had already suggested. Bucke left Bolton for a few days with Tennyson returning with Edward Carpenter on August 24th 1891. Whitman readings, walks around Rivington, and night-long discussions follcwed. Wallace decided he would go to America and sailec a few days later from Liverpool.

Walt Whitman and Warren Fritzinger on Camden Wharf. Photo by Dr John Johnston, taken during his visit in 1890.

Wallace's impressions of Whitman were recorded with equal detail to Johnston's. On arrival at the Whitman household Whitman greeted him with "So you've come to be disillusioned have you!" and Wallace did later confess to not seeing what he had expected. Rather than meeting a towering majestic figure, here was :

".....an infirm old man, unaffectedly simple and gentle in manner, giving me courteous and affectionate welcome on terms of perfect equality, and reminding me far more of the common humanity found everywhere rather than suggesting any singular eminence or special distinction."

Much of the chat was commonplace, interspersed with comments on other writers, the state of America and the activity of the Bolton group. Wallace stayed with the Traubels, becoming close friends with Horace and Anne. He visited other Whitmanites such as Gilchrist, Harned and Josef Fels the socialist soap manufacturer.

On Wallace's return, the correspondence with both Whitman himself and Traubel increased, in spite of Whitman's deteriorating health. On 6th February 1892 he wrote to Johnston that he was 'deadly weak' but was able to announce the publication of the 1892 edition of "Leaves of Grass", for him the definitive one. He ended by sending his thanks to the Bolton group "which may be my last." However, he wrote the following day:

"Same condition continued – more and more it comes to the fore that the only theory worthy of our modern times for great literature, politics and sociology must combine all the bulk-people of all lands, the women not forgetting. But the mustard plaster on my side is stinging and I must stop. Good bye to all."

Traubel kept Bolton informed of his condition, and was instructed by Whitman to send his best wishes, adding: "I am no saint. Don't let our Bolton fellows tumble into that bog." He died on 26th March, holding Traubel's hand.

Whitman's regard for the Bolton group seemed surprising to some commentators. Traubel recorded a conversation between Gilchrist and Whitman, when Gilchrist said: "It suprises me that you should be so taken with those Bolton folks – they're not famous in England at all." Whitman caustically replied "It suprises you does it? Well I've had my be lyfull of famous people! Thank God they're just nobody at all, like all people who are worthwhile."

(in "The Conservator" March 1918)

For Whitman, the Bolton group represented 'the common people' whom he aimed at, despite the few manual workers amongst them. None of them had literary pretensions and most did mundane clerical jobs. Whitman was genuinely delighted to have their support and to a degree they made up for the lack of recognition amongst most American workers in his lifetime.

The Bolton – America links forged during the 1890s remained strong up to the late 1950s. Although Horace Traubel died in 1919, Anne Traubel maintained her contacts with the Bolton group, being especially close to Minnie Whiteside. On 5th July 1953, she wrote to Minnie:

"......as our precious day approaches, I write these few words to bring us nearer to each other and to refresh our thoughts in the sunshine of unfolding love."

In the 1930s, several Whitman scholars such as Prof. Will S. Monroe visited Bolton, and were entertained by the surviving Whitmanites. John Burroughs and Clara Barras also came over to speak in Bolton, at St. George's Congregational Church. Verne Dyson of the Walt Whitman Birthplace Association wrote to Minnie Whiteside on 14th June 1959 saying :

"We think of you often – you and your rich memories of the past, so full of recollections of Walt, Wallace and other members of the blessed circle, blessed and eternal."

Horace Traubel (1893).

6. SPREADING THE GOSPEL

The visits and correspondence with Whitman did give the Bolton group a certain status within parts of the local labour movement. However, Wallace had to work very hard at convincing the great socialist figures like Blatchford and Hardie that this American poet had something to say. The Bolton group's own socialist politics were formed in the early 1890s as the Labour Church and Independent Labour Party established themselves in the town. James Sims was the central figure in the Labour Church, and became the movement's national president: he was a good friend of Allen Clarke who often came to the meetings. William Broadhurst was an important later member of the Whitman group, and he describes here how he first met the Whitmanites at Bolton Labour Church......

"Membership in it was not dependent on any declaration of faith. It had no set theological tenets. The service consisted of a recital of the Lord's Prayer, the singing together of some democratic songs, called hymns, and a lecture by some man or woman who was in the vanguard of democratic thought..............Fred Wild and Wentworth Dixon were active members and one Sunday evening, lo! Wallace was there. Sims introduced me and I passed into the shelter of Wallace's wing."

(W. Broadhurst: Address delivered at Swan Hotel, 6th December 1930)

Alice Collinge was an especially important later member of the group who first came into contact with the Whitmanites at the Labour Church. In her autobiographical notes she records her debt to Sarah Reddish for introducing her into socialist activity and recalls how 'the socialism of that day claimed me'. She mentions how, in her 'humble role at the piano' she heard 'such people as Mrs Despard, Margaret Macmillan, Edward Carpenter, Mrs Bruce Glasier' and others.

Charles Sixsmith came into contact with the Bolton Whitmanites in the early 1890s through socialist activity. He was employed at Bentinck Mill, Moses Gate, and eventually became managing director. He was a major figure in the Independent Labour Party and later in Bolton Clarion Cycling Club. He lived at Brownlow, Adlington from 1908 and was elected a rural district councillor in 1910 – eventually becoming chairman of the council in Chorley.

Carpenter and the Bolton Group

Edward Carpenter was the first major socialist figure whom the Bolton group met, in 1891. It was the occasion of Bucke's second visit. Wallace, Johnston and Sixsmith visited Carpenter for a weekend at his home at Millthorpe, in the hills above Sheffield, in August 1892. They spent the weekend talking, walking and listening to Carpenter playing Beethoven sonatas on the piano. An interesting exchange took place between Wallace and Carpenter on socialism:

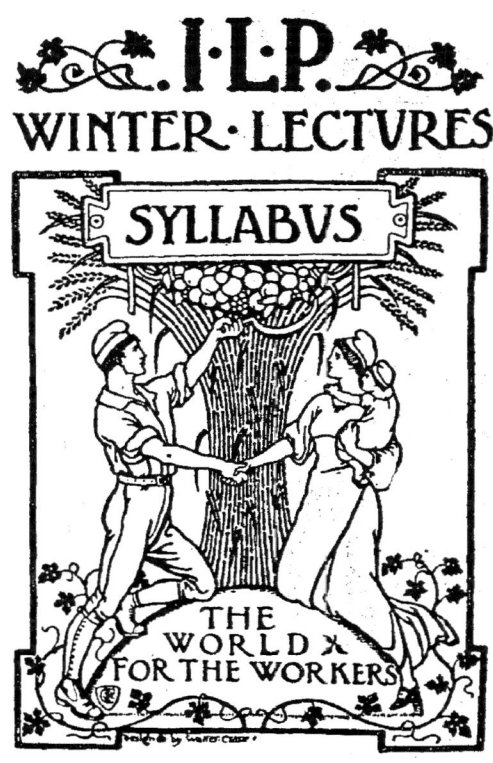

.I.L.P.
WINTER·LECTVRES

SYLLABVS

THE
WORLD
FOR THE WORKERS

NEW·PRINCES·THEATRE
BLACKBVRN · 1910-11.

Blackburn ILP's Winter Syllabus including visits from Edward Carpenter, J. Bruce Glasier, and Mrs Charlotte Despard.

Carpenter (back, centre) caressing Sixsmith's leg, with Charles Merrill at the front. George Hukin to the left of the picture.

"Referring to socialism I said that I accepted and rejoiced in the socialistic spirit, but that I could not accept socialism as a formula, as a theory of government. He (Carpenter) said that strictly speaking, that was his own case too, he was more of an anarchist than anything else as regards government. But, one could not rest in abstractions. To descend into the practical arena it was necessary to work with people whose opinions differed from one's own."

(Notes of a Visit to Edward Carpenter, 13th – 15th August 1892)

Carpenter was a frequent visitor to Bolton, often speaking at the Labour Church and combining this with a visit to the Bolton group. He wrote to Wallace on 28th March 1894 saying he was giving a lecture in Bolton on "The Future Society" and would call.

Johnston and Sixsmith became particularly close friends of Carpenter, both spending holidays abroad with him and his lover George Merrill. Johnston visited Millthorpe frequently in the 1890s and his diary records animated discussion on socialism, spiritualism and mysticism, sexuality and clairvoyance. Sixsmith began visiting from about 1898 onwards, becoming a lifelong friend of both Carpenter and Merrill. He gave Carpenter much support when he was being hounded by a local bigot called O'Brien who attempted to stir up feeling about Carpenter's homosexuality. Sixsmith also acted as secretary for the 70th birthday celebration for Carpenter.

Carpenter with Johnston (to his left) and Merrill right.

Carpenter found the Bolton group a bit strange. He greeted them on one occasion with the words:

"I have seen a lot of your society for some years and I have seen a good deal of societies of the socialistic order and coming here tonight it makes me feel that there is something at work here. I do not know whether you embrace the socialist ideal or not but I feel that your spirit is in essence the same as theirs."

(undated – probably c. 1900)

Carpenter did more than anyone nationally to spread Walt Whitman's poetry and ideals, but he did recognise the role of the Bolton group, despite their eccentricities:

If there was a somewhat Pickwickian note about its revels still no one could doubt the sincerity of its enthusiasm. It helped largely to spread the study and appreciation of Whitman's work in the north of England."

(Edward Carpenter "My Days and Dreams".)

Katherine Conway – Bruce Glasier

Katherine Conway was one of the most popular figures in the early socialist movement and was especially close to the Bolton Whitmanites. Her first contact with the group was in 1893 when she came to speak at the ILP's newly opened Labour Institute on Bowker's Row, on the subject of "Liberalism – True and False'. Dr Johnston recorded in his diary for 10th March that she "made a marvellous speech, interspersed with readings from Whitman". The vote of thanks was moved by Whitmanite Sam Hodgkinson who had recently joined the ILP ranks. The college gave her an escort to the station – Wallace, Johnston, Wild, Hodgkinson and Greenhalgh. After her departure Wallace was misty-eyed about her. Johnston records him saying: "Well, I've had a thoroughly happy day – she is a splendid woman and the communion with her is such as she is the best sermon in the world."

Katherine Conway (Glasier).

Katherine was soon in regular correspondence with the group, particularly with Wallace, from her home at the short-lived socialist colony at Starnthwaite Mill, near Kendal. In May 1893 she wrote to the Bolton 'comrades':

"Dear comrades,

That is his word, Walt Whitman's, and I use it fearlessly. As I understand it, like the disciples of old, you are meeting together after the death of him you know as your leader, that you may strengthen each other's faith in his gospel, gain a fuller understanding of its vast issues and learn together how best to send it forth to the nations............"

Katherine's associations with Bolton continued for the rest of her lifetime: with Minnie Whiteside and ILP friends like the Rowlands, until she died in 1950. Katherine married Bruce Glasier – probably second only to Keir Hardie in the ILP leadership. Though Wallace seems to have been personally hurt by the marriage, it was also a good opportunity to further spread the Whitman gospel, and they became close friends.

Through Glasier, Wallace became an influential figure in the ILP and addressed several ILP conferences on the ideas of Whitman. In Katherine's obituary for Wallace in the "Labour Leader" she wrote:

"Bruce and I, and Keir Hardie, and most itinerant ILP lecturers have known and stayed in his home since 1892........he had a wonderful power of sustaining sympathy. He always knew when Keir or Bruce were in a tight place in the fight, and his letter never failed to come with just the right message of cheer........."

("Labour Leader" January 1926)

Others acknowledged how Wallace's home was used as a sort of socialist convalescent home for weary 'ILP evangelists'.

In the 1900s Wallace sided with Glasier, Hardie and Ramsey Macdonald in their attempts to steer the ILP away from an alliance with the Marxist Social Democratic Federation, and towards the non-socialist trade union leaders. In a revealing letter to Bruce on 15th February 1909 Wallace urged Glasier to stick to his editorship of "Labour Leader" despite attacks from ILP members 'untypical' of the majority:

" The typical ILP socialist is very different from the rest.....he is usually a worker in contact with the actualities of working life and their divine lessons, combining idealism with practical sagacity and with sympathetic appreciation of different points of view, with broad humanity, unselfishness.............and people of this type are exactly those who cannot fail and do not fail to recognise the qualities of your work on "The Leader".

Bruce is compared to Abraham Lincoln – 'personally degraded and vilified' – and then Wallace attacks the SDF in terms that had by then become familiar in the ILP:

"Sincere in their way, narrow, intolerant, unregenerate, selfish, repellent. Socialism will never come from them.... folks who accept socialism as a theory, but whose desire for its violent proclamation and partial realisation is curiously proportioned to the absence of its real spirit in themselves, and to whom it is simply an offset to the tedium of conventional lives spent to worldly and selfish ends."

In the latter category he includes the "Clarion" readers from whom he once expected so much. The letter is a sad commentary on the journey of ethical socialism from the idealism of the 1890s to the practical social reformism and compromise of the 1900s, despite Wallace's hopes of "The Labour Leader" 'organising the movement to practical ends and setting it marching to its destiny' – through a coalition of trades unionists and socialists.

By 1919 it was clear that Bruce was dying of cancer. Wallace was deeply upset and helped him through his last months with letters and Whitman poems – including "In Death's Valley". His final demise in 1920 led to greater contact with Katherine and a much stronger political correspondence between the two. The experience of the First World War had pushed both of them further to the left, and as we shall see later, Wallace and Katherine formed that part of the ILP which supported the Russian Revolution in opposition to Snowden and Macdonald.

Robert Blatchford and "The Clarion"

Blatchford, by 1895, regarded Whitman as one of the central influences on northern socialism. The conversion did not happen overnight. A year before hailing Whitman as the 'trumpet-tongued titan' of democracy he was writing to Wallace suggesting he hadn't even read his works:

"Thank you very much for the Whitman book. I have not had time to read it yet and God knows when I shall. There is so much to do and I seem to get drawn deeper and deeper by the drift of the tide of politics......Here am I as much adrift as a cork in the river. I have no idea where fate shall carry me. Bah! All imagination! All idle moping and sentimental nonsense. But some things we know are real. The ugly things are real. The slums, the sweater, the factories and mines.....and so the dog comes back to his kennel and growls and shows his teeth as duty bids."

(Blatchford to Wallace 23rd August 1894)

Wallace's reply, on receipt of Blatchford's letter, tells him to marry his concern for social evils with an idealism derived from Whitman's message of comradeship:

"Your dissatisfaction for yourself – as of a dog growling in a kennel – is due to your growing need for, and reaching towards, 'the word final', the 'key', the solution to your problems. If only I could convey it to you!............Your work (noble as it is) for what you foolishly call 'the real things' (as if they alone were real) will be better done: for, in addition to its devotion and comradeship, it will be filled with infinite hope and unshakeable peace."

Wallace met Blatchford in Bolton the following week, at a concert arranged by Allen Clarke. Relations improved and Blatchford adopted Whitmanism, as we saw in "The New Religion in the North", twelve months after the correspondence with Wallace. What caused the dislike of Blatchford in later times, evidenced by his letter to Bruce Glasier in 1909? Probably a combination of Blatchford's increasing jingoism, which lost him many friends (including Allen Clarke) and his own blend of 'materialism' which discounted the spiritual realm which Wallace saw as crucial. To Blatchford, Whitman was just a good poet; to Wallace he was a prophet of a new era. However, Blatchford's espousal of Whitman in the 1890s – when he

Robert Blatchford.

was at his peak of popularity and "The Clarion" was read by tens of thousands – must have led many socialists to Whitman's work. Perhaps we have Wallace to thank for this.

Caroline Martyn

"Carrie Martyn" was a revered figure in northern socialism in the 1890s; many who heard her speak suggest she carried an almost religious sense of inspiration. She was naturally inclined to the semi-mystical works of Whitman and became a close friend of the Bolton group before her sad death in 1896. This description of her speaking at the

Bolton mill village of Eagley captures the impression she made on many:

"In company with some two or three hundred people I listened to an exposition of socialist principles, illustrated with the sayings and doings of the Carpenter of Nazareth. My wonder at what seemed the intrepidy of a young and defenceless woman turned to amazement at myself that I had never seen things in this light before. She had spoken as no woman had ever spoken before in my hearing. Scales fell from my eyes, and ere long I was a socialist."

(Lena Wallis "The Life and Letters of Caroline Martyn)

Allen Clarke also remembers her with affection, speaking on the sands at Blackpool "her voice by the blue sea in the sunshine of a golden day, pleading for the fallen, forsaken and oppressed."

Her association with the Bolton group began in 1893. She stayed at Wallace's on several occasions and her love for him is shown in the following letter written on 6th July 1894, whilst she was living in Newton Heath, Manchester. It also shows the strain she was under at the time, with speaking engagements at Ashton, Salford, Tottington, north Manchester and Farnworth, in less than a week:

"The knowledge of your recollection and brotherly love is a very real help to me; your letters, your expression of true sympathy are a tonic. I hope and believe I am doing very practical work for the cause of our prophet, that the reforms I advocate, the ideals I so feebly teach, are the same that he would advocate today..........I came home from the lecture very, very tired and am writing in order to settle my nerves before I try to sleep. Whitman's teaching has brought me not the capacity to love, but the strength to express it. I do not suppose that I am separate from you, I am no more myself than you are............"

Within two years she was dead from an attack of pneumonia whilst organising the women jute workers in Dundee. Her last surviving note to the Bolton group was written on 18th August 1895:

"Only the universal love of the mother-heart can compass the world's woe, only the all-embracing tenderness of the mother-voice can soothe the world's sorrow, only the all-embracing sympathy of mother-care can provide for the world's needs. The world shall be saved by its mothers."

Keir Hardie

Wallace badgered Keir Hardie into becoming a Whitmanite. He visited the Bolton group on several occasions. The correspondence began in 1892, with Wallace despatching copies of "Leaves of Grass" to the great man. Hardie made an evasive reply on 29th December, admitting a certain fondness for the poet though his reading had been limited. The two men were temperamentally suited and became good friends. He wrote to Wallace on 24th December breaking out of his usual reticence:

Keir Hardie

Greeting card from Keir Hardie to the Bolton Group, New year, 1893,

"Thanks for your letters. It is not mine to make a show of my feelings, and for that reason am supposed to be void of them. If I don't reciprocate in words your kind message, it is not that I don't appreciate it."

Like Glasier, Hardie got Wallace's support in his fight against the ILP left in the 1900s; Hardie was perhaps less committed to the compromising policy that Macdonald was pushing and still less keen on parliamentary life, as suggested by a letter to Wallace on Commons notepaper, sometime between 1900 and 1902:

"..........oftener than once, I have been on the point of applying for the Chiltern Hundreds (ie resigning – PS) and having done with it. At such times I make for the country and try to gather fresh courage. To resign would be so misunderstood and might do much harm."

In the Whitman Collection in Bolton Library are numerous other letters from Hardie, giving an insight into this revered figure of the labour movement. This note from his home in Cumnock shows a more relaxed side to him:

"I have been in the garden all day weeding and hoeing. The song of the birds is in my ears and some of nature's music in my soul"

Wider Contacts: John Addington Symonds and AE (George Russell)

As well as corresponding with leading figures within the British labour movement and the American Whitman comrades, the Bolton group was in touch with kindred souls in other parts of the world. Chief among these were John Addington Symonds, the British classics scholar who made Davos, Switzerland his home, and George Russell, known in much of his writing as AE, the Irish writer, mystic and co-operator.

Both Johnston and Wallace corresponded with Symonds as part of an international Whitmanite circle which included Horace Traubel in America, Carpenter, Johnston and Wallace in Britain as well as others like Havelock Ellis who were involved in sexual research. Symonds was himself a homosexual who also lived a 'normal' married life.

On 19th December 1892 he wrote to Wallace about his almost completed "Study of Walt Whitman" and also refers to a prosecution against a homosexual in Bolton, and asks Wallace for information on it. Several of the illustrations in his "Study" were photographs taken by Johnston on his visit to Whitman. The correspondence continued right up to Symonds' death in April 1893. One of his last letters was a note to Wallace on the publication of his "Study of Walt Whitman". For further aspects of the correspondence see the chapter on "Personal Relations".

AE is a later contact and quite how the correspondence began is not clear. We do know Wallace had an interest in Irish politics and AE was probably especially attractive on account of his mystical brand of socialism. One of the the peripheral Whitmanites, Will Hayes, was a devoted follower of Patrick Pearse and Sinn Fein and may have intorduced Russell to the Bolton Group.

The first surviving letter from AE was written on 27th August 1919 and is about 'Irish bibliophiles'. Later letters, written during the War of Independence, express AE's support for Irish freedom coupled with a desire to see a democratic and non-sectarian independent republic. During the war, AE saw many of the co-operative creameries he had pioneered razed to the ground by the Black and Tans and reflected to Wallace:

21st April 1921:

"Too many sensations destroy one's sensitiveness and the horrible thing happens that we begin to regard shootings, raids, wreckings, burnings, all as normal."

As the war dragged on, AE put his hopes in Michael Collins and a negotiated settlement with Britain based on the Treaty of 1922. Instead, Collins was shot and a bloody civil war followed. AE wrote an open letter in which he tried to overcome the post-treaty bitterness, but admitted defeat:

"I am afraid we are in for a bad time, but we shall climb out of it. I never lose faith in the Irish genius, but it has to be educated, and that takes a long time."

(Letter to Wallace 4th June 1923)

The correspondence between AE and Wallace provides a fascinating glimpse of Ireland struggling to free itself from British rule, and the problems it found itself in after the signing of the treaty – in particular the starvation of cultural life in the late 1920s as a conservative government allied with the church to stamp on anything remotely controversial.

Portrait of George Russell (AE) by Hilda Roberts, 1930.

7. PERSONAL RELATIONS

Perhaps the most remarkable thing about the Bolton group was the intensity of their personal relations. This was in an age when men were expected to make little show of their feelings – especially to members of the same sex. Six years after Wallace died, Anne Traubel wrote to Minnie Whiteside expressing her belief that "the college has been unmatched in my experience as a centre of love and comradeship".

Nearly forty years earlier, Wallace had written to his friends about the basis of the group:

"Let no man hang back in dread or doubt!................it is for us to do as Walt did – to proclaim that man includes all distinctions and diversities – that brotherhood and comradeship applies to all men...........that love binds all and that God lies hid in the heart of the meanest."

(Letter to Eagle Street College 6th January 1893)

Wallace is talking about being more than 'just good friends'. At the 1923 Whitman Day Celebration he takes the "Calamus" poems as his theme. He insists that 'the love of comrades' which Whitman celebrates represents 'the deepest assurance of spiritual life and immortality'. He continues:

"It is obvious that the love of comrades is vitally different from the tepid feeling that passes for friendship. And the love of comrades is immeasurably more than the mere desire for companionship in hours of leisure or recreation. It is the vital and enduring bond – deep as life – which unites kindred souls on their road to God in co-operation for ideal ends."

(Whitman Day Address 31st May 1923)

> Anderton, near Chorley.
> Lancashire, England.
> 15 March 1892
>
> Dear Walt,
>
> Just a line a too my dearest friend, my comrade & father, dearest of all to my soul, to express the triumph & joy & cheer with which I think of you & with which I receive tidings of you. Outwardly sad enough, but deep within my soul I know that all is well, & that our last words should be triumph & praise.
>
> Day by day I think of you with tenderest sympathy & love. If only I could come for a moment to your bedside & imprint upon your lips a long & loving kiss. Be it as if I *were* with you, & here upon the paper I send you one as a token of my dearest love X
>
> Wallace

Wallace's last letter to Whitman, March 15th 1892.

Emma Goldman's 'Mother Earth' – advertising an unusual society event and leading with verses from Whitman.

Dr Johnston was equally interested in the themes of 'manly love' in "Calamus". Between 1890 and 1893 he was in regular correspondence with Symonds, who found practical expression of this love with Swiss peasants and a Venetian gondolier. Writing to Johnston on 12th January 1891 he asks:

"I wonder what more the "Calamus" contains, whether the luminous ideal of chivalry based on brotherhood and manly affection will ever be realised."

For Symonds this ideal excludes women by definition. In a letter to Carpenter, pro- feminist and gay, he suggests that women should be restricted to rearing the children and doing household chores.

Wallace himself has little to say about women, unlike his idol who – unusual for his time – usually refers to both men and women. It is idle to speculate to what extent Wallace and other members of the group were practising homosexuals – there seems little doubt that a lot of their activity was based around a more or less sublimated homosexuality, even though many of them were married. They accepted Carpenter's open relationship with George Merrill in a way that many socialists at that time didn't. On Wallace's first visit to Carpenter, he commented on George:

"Merrill is a young fellow, simple, natural, gentle, a compositor on "The Weekly Telegraph" and it was pleasant to observe the perfectly free, simple and affectionate relationship between Carpenter and him."

("Notes of a Visit to Edward Carpenter" August 1892)

Johnston, in a later visit, mentions Merrill being 'deeply in love' with Carpenter and 'womanly as any woman'. The doctor records his amusement at Merrill's jealousy for his lover which sometimes 'reached the point of hysteria'.

On a visit in 1898, Johnston discussed the question of homosexuality with Carpenter and the prosecution case over Havelock Ellis' book (Ellis was a sexual reformer):

"……..discuss Ellis' 'Sexual Inversion' and legal proceedings. He is intensely interested in the subject of 'sexual inversion', so am I. I think he likes to get me to discuss the subject as there are so few with whom he can do so."

In this diary entry (for 1898) the above words 'so am I' had been partially erased – perhaps the doctor was covering his tracks?

Sixsmith, who accompanied Wallace and Johnston on the first visit to Carpenter, is the most ambiguous of the group, and clearly bi-sexual. He was married and had children, and outraged his neighbours by lovemaking in the garden. However, in an undated letter to Carpenter (probably around 1895-9) he expresses some of the emotional dilemmas of a respectable young man being more than a bit unsure of his feelings:

"Yes dear friend, I do at times feel very restless, with an aching longing after something, and a feeling of great loneliness. I have many sad, sad, days, fretful (even to the point of tears)……………I could give all for something my heart craves, which I get many glimpses cf, but no full response. You are surely right – love is what life is for…………..But my love affairs have broken down and I have not found the true mate. Women attract me, and yet full intercourse has not satisfied me, and I prefer the company of men, and can be attracted to them also. But really I am the greatest puzzle to myself, a bundle of paradoxes and contradictions."

Sixsmith had an affair with Philip Dalmas, a young American who stayed with Carpenter in 1894. He was credited with mystical powers – he claimed to hear flowers and identify colours from musical sounds. In a brief note dated 25th December 1894 he tells Sixsmith "I love you very much dear boy". He adds some disparaging remarks about Wallace, including a suggestion that he should be blown up! He ends: "Much love to you Charlie, Ever your true, Phil D".

What strikes the reader of correspondence between the group was their demonstrably affectionate terms, and frequent ending of letters with 'much love', 'with deepest love' etc, terms which even today most men would feel uncomfortable with in letters from the same sex.

Wallace and Katherine

Wallace was close to Katherine Glasier for many years – he seems to have fallen in love with her at their first meeting in 1893, and wanted her to be some sort of 'spirit wife'. In the end she opted for a more conventional relationship with Bruce Glasier – to Wallace's evident annoyance. An irate letter was sent off which caused her to complain to Bruce:

"I think Whitman would have horse-whipped him for his letter to me this morning. Oh Bruce – if I had gone into slavery with him and then met thee!

(Quoted in L. Thompson "The Enthusiasts")

After the initial recriminations, friendship was re-established, though on a less intense level until Bruce's death in 1920. The relationship was both emotional and political. Wallace and Katherine both became concerned at the rightward drift of the ILP in the '20s under Snowden and Macdonald. As well as her lecturing for the ILP, Katherine became editor of "The Labour Leader", the ILP's paper, after Bruce's death. In 1916 Wallace had strongly backed her support for the Dublin Easter Rising – a position many in the ILP baulked at. He wrote congratulating an article of hers:

"The paragraph on Ireland is ……………first rate…………..in its praise of the high dedication of brave hearts who have died for Ireland, in its reference to the damning poverty and degradation of the workers of Dublin…………..the economic conditions which are the real cause of the unrest which will yet issue in revolution. For Ireland still preserves her soul inviolate – as England and Scotland do not."

Probably the last sentence was a reference to their involvement in the War and in the suppression of the Rising.

A year later Russia was in the throes of a revolution and the ILP enthusiastically supported it – at first. Later Snowden became violently anti-Bolshevik, along with his wife Ethel. Wallace remained unflinching in his support, and wrote to Katherine on 30th December 1918:

"My own opinion is that Russia is the standard bearer of a new democratic advance of incalculable value to all the world."

Katherine shared Wallace's pro-Soviet stance and became increasingly concerned at Snowden's attacks. Crisis was reached when, in 1920, British forces were poised to invade the Soviet Republic. Snowden submitted a particularly virulent piece which in effect supported the intervention, for publication in "Labour Leader". Though Katherine was editor, Snowden had overall control. The article went in, but Katherine added a disclaimer. There was the predictable uproar, and Katherine was edged out of the editor's seat. Her diary for April 1920 makes sad reading:

April 6th: Utterly alone at office. Break down and end my Labour Leader days.

April 7th: Go to Macclesfield in despair to tramp with Glen (her son)

By the end of April she arrives at Wallace's and begins a steady recovery from her mauling in the ILP. They go for walks round Rivington and the moors. On 22nd April she records having 'a wonderful time' with Minnie and Glen. During this period at Wallace's she seems to have undergone a form of spiritual renewal akin to Wallace's 'illumination' in 1885. On 25th April she wrote: "At last I understand – I know I am deathless". On 10th November she records: "Walk to Lake (ie Rivington) – I have cosmic consciousness of my own"

Her recovery allowed her to get back on the road as a lecturer both for the ILP and the Workers Educational Association; the visits to Wallace continued and they remained 'loving comrades' until Wallace's death in January 1926. The obituary in "Labour Leader" was written by Katherine and records her debt to him.

Philip Snowden.

J. Bruce Glasier.

8. TOWARDS THE DAWN

Wallace owed a great deal to Katherine; without her political guidance Wallace could have become a mystical crank. Instead, he was able to wed his Whitmanism to a viable socialist politics that enriched each other. Whereas many 'ethical socialists' such as Philip Snowden ("St Philip of Blackburn") moved to the right in the complex world facing socialists after 1914, Wallace and Katherine were radicalised further. For both of them, the Irish Uprising, Russia, British poverty and unemployment were part of the 'world crisis' that would be resolved by a socialism based on Whitman's ethics.

In his 'last political will and testament', delivered to Bolton W.E.A. on 16th October 1920 he traces the degeneration of capitalist society, but with it the rise of new literary and religious forces; spiritualism, free thought and a new interest in the west for Buddhism. Alongside this, there were new political forces arising:

"Concurrently with this development there has been a gradual awakening of the democratic spirit amongst the masses..............the more thoughtful amongst them recognising the injustice and many evils of the system, and uniting in various movements for their removal and for the establishment of socialism, communism or anarchism."

A superb picture of the group in the 1920s at Ormrod's house. Wild and Ormrod are at the rear. Alice Collinge is seated at the extreme right of the picture.

He says that the capitalist class will fight to the end to defend their rule and will:

"........stoop to any crime or infamy to gain their predatory ends, even though it may involve the destruction or starvation of millions of men, women and children."

Despite their control of the army, navy, airforce, police and the press, a force was arising, such as in Russia, 'in whom they see a spectre tenfold more dread to them than Banquo's ghost to Macbeth.' Before long, ends Wallace, democracy and socialism will triumph and Whitman's ideas will come into their own:

"When human brotherhood and international solidarity are generally recognised – as they will be in the new era towards which we are advancing, even through the wide chaos and numberless miseries of today and the great social convulsions yet to come, Walt Whitman will increasingly be recognised as its greatest pioneer and ever new depths of wisdom and beauty will be found in his 'mystic, deep, unfathomable songs'."

Wallace remained active in the early 1920s and the end came quite suddenly on January 16th 1926. He died of a ruptured appendix. Announcing Wallace's death, John Ormrod (a keen Bolton Wanderers supporter) spoke of his 'transfer and promotion' to a higher realm.

With Johnston in failing health and exiled to Bispham, the leadership of the 'first generation' of Bolton Whitmanites had been removed. Or, as they might have said, had moved on....

Whitman Fruit Cocktail! A heady mix.

9. LAST OF THE WHITMANITES?

Wallace's death removed the fountain-head of the group. Johnston died a year later in 1927, though he had been an invalid for some time previously. Fred Wild, describing himself as 'the last of the Mohicans', helped to keep the group together until his death in 1935. However, the spur for continuing the Whitman Day Celebration was taken up by Minnie Whiteside, John Ormrod, Alice Collinge and William Broadhurst. These formed the core of the 'second generation' of Bolton Whitmanites.

The annual event continued to take place at Walker Fold, at least up to the 1950s. Katherine Glasier kept in touch with the group through Minnie and continued to visit her. Both Minnie and John Ormrod kept in contact with the American Whitman community: Anne Traubel, Clara Barrus and her partner John Burroughs (the latter only up to the 1930s), as well as Whitman scholars like Verne Dyson and Charles E. Feinberg. Ormrod became close friends with the Traubel family and in the final years of the group hosted meetings at his house on Walker Fold. He and his wife celebrated their 60th wedding anniversary on April 21st 1959.

Bolton people in their various ways kept the flame flickering. Frank Singleton, then editor of the Bolton Evening News, used his 'Editor's Notebook' of July 16th 1958 to reproduce a review of Wallace and Johnston's 'Visits to Walt Whitman in 1890-1' by Virginia Woolf. It was originally published in the 'Times Literary Supplement' on January 3rd 1918. Successive Bolton Chief Librarians have maintained an intense pride in the collection, recognising what a priceless treasure it was. Bolton branch of the W.E.A. maintained interest and a photograph in the collection of the Walt Whitman Birthplace on Long Island shows an early 1960s group displaying a copy of 'Leaves of Grass', with early TV set in the background.

As various members of the group passed on, Bolton Library steadily built up a collection second to none in this country. The libraries of Johnston and Wallace were vast and most of the material is now in the safekeeping of the Public Library, along with the various items of Whitmania such as the canary bird and loving cup. Much of the original correspondence from Whitman was sent back to the US Library of Congress. There is also a large collection, from the estate of Charles Sixsmith, in John Rylands Library, in Manchester.

The continuity of the group took a long time to break: probably the death of John Ormrod in the early 1960s brought it to an end. The links with American Whitman scholars continued through the Public Library, with fairly regular contacts between Bolton and Duke's University in Detroit, and Wayne State University. These links eventually came to an end.

In 1984, writing in the first edition of this book, I said "...it is to be hoped that with a renewed interest amongst Bolton people in their Whitman heritage some of the links can quickly be re-forged. Next year, 1985, will be exactly a hundred years since Wallace and the "Eagle Street College" first celebrated Whitman's birthday. I hope Bolton will mark the centenary in a suitable manner".

And of course they did, and a new generation of 'Whitmanites' came about. There is still quite a bit of life left in them. The next chapter brings the story up to date.

A rare photograph of a Bolton W.E.A. class on Whitman, taken in the 1960s. (From Whitman Birthplace Museum, Long Island).

10. THE THIRD GENERATION OF BOLTON WHITMANITES

Bolton Peoples History

The revival of local interest in Bolton's connections with Whitman came through members of Bolton Socialist Club. This was highly appropriate, given Wallace and Johnston's socialist principles and personal contacts with members of the Club in the 1890s though neither seem to have been directly connected to the Socialist Club.

The Club started a series of talks in 1983 under the general banner of 'Bolton People's History' and stimulated interest in Bolton's radical past. The catalyst for the Whitman revival came about through a reading of Allen Clarke's 'Moorlands and Memories', where reference to Whitman and his Bolton connections was made (see introductory essay).

Ed Folsom of Iowa, nonchalantly carries the loving cup on Whitman Day 1985, followed by Denis Pye with bike.

The staff of Bolton Library, including the Chief Librarian, Norman Parker, Barry Mills, Kevin Campbell and Viv Brown were incredibly helpful in helping me delve into the collection. At the time, most of the correspondence was in boxes, largely uncatalogued. But what a treasure trove it was, with original letters from Keir Hardie, Edward Carpenter, Robert Blatchford, AE and many other major figures in the early socialist movement.

The first revived Whitman Day took place on June 2nd 1984 with a lecture in Bolton Library and a display of the Library's Whitman collection. This includes a first edition of 'Leaves of Grass' (there are only two other known copies) and other artefacts including the stuffed canary. This was followed by a bus ride to Barrow Bridge and a walk up the '59 steps' to Walker Fold. We were allowed to bring the loving cup, presented to the Bolton group by New York Whitmanite J.H. Johnston when his namesake Dr Johnston visited in 1894. Although the traditional spiced claret was not available, a bottle of red wine from a local off licence sufficed. Readings from Whitman were given by several members of the group before we adjourned to the tea rooms at Brian Hey for scones and jam.

The Bolton Evening News reported the event thus:

'Lilac Squad Revive Odd Day of Tribute'

'Poetry buffs in Bolton will gather lilacs every Spring-time after the successful unearthing of a bizarre century-old tradition. Literature lovers have decided to make Whitman Day – an odd celebration of the American poet's birthday – an annual fixture. About 30 people met in the town over the weekend to honour Whitman and relive the acts of an eccentric group of working class intellectuals who forged close links with him at the turn of the century. Like their predecessors they wore sprigs of lilac and took to the moors for open-air recitals, passing round a two-pint 'loving cup' – a gift bequeathed from the great man himself.'

Good job no-one mentioned the stuffed canary.

The 1985 event included a visit from Ed Folsom, one of the leading US Whitman scholars. Greetings were received from William White in the United States and from Geoff Sill, President of the Walt Whitman Association.

Sill stressed Whitman's message of universal peace, brotherhood and love and concluded his message with the words 'We are glad to play some part in keeping his vision alive and share that joy with you on this day.'

In 1986 socialist feminist Sheila Rowbotham was a special guest, braving the torrential moorland rain. Subsequent years have seen the usual unpredictable Lancashire weather, veering from cold rain to warm, almost balmy

A diverse group of '3rd Generation' Whitmanites outside 40 Babylon Lane – Whitman Day 2002.

days where the group lounged in the meadows whilst passing round the loving cup, entertained by impromptu readings from Whitman.

Another Boltonian's visit

Publication of 'Loving Comrades' was followed by the author's trip to the United States in Summer 1985, to look through Whitman archives in New York, Washington, Philadelphia and California. It was an opportunity to establish links with several leading figures in Whitman studies, including Whitman biographer Gay Wilson Allen as well as meeting Ed Folsom in Iowa. I was privileged to meet, and almost share a glass of whisky with, Charles E. Feinberg and meet the daughter of John Burrows, Mrs Elizabeth Burroughs-Kelley at her 'Riverby' home in the Catskills. Mrs Burroughs-Kelley was particularly pleased to welcome me on July 23rd 1985 – 95 years to the day since Johnston's visit to Burroughs at Riverby. I met Gay Wilson Allen at his New Jersey home. Everyone was astonishingly friendly and welcoming.

The trip took in some extensive train journeys across America, from New York to Washington, back to Philadelphia then across the continent, via Iowa City and the Folsoms, to Berkeley, California. It included a shorter trip from New York up to Buffalo and Niagara Falls. One of the most poignant visits was to the former soap works of Joseph Fels on the outskirts of Philadelphia. The demolition of the works was almost complete. I wondered how many people realised the irony of this great capitalist enterprise helping to bankroll not only the American socialist movement, but also the Independent Labour Party in Britain?

Some of the itinerary followed in the steps of Wallace and Johnston's visits. Whitman's house at 330 Mickle Street, Camden, New Jersey was the sole surviving building in the area, surrounded by urban dereliction. The horrors of inner city Camden were balanced by the warmth of my welcome at the Whitman House by curator Eleanor Ray. On the mantelpiece was a photo of Wallace, and nearby a parasol presented to Whitman by Johnston on his visit in 1890. I was similarly welcomed at the Whitman Birthplace Museum at Huntington, Long Island. This is a classic US commuter settlement, complete with a 'Walt Whitman Shopping Mall'.

Bolton Socialist Club: a long tradition of nonconformity

The Whitman link would have died if it were not for the members of Bolton Socialist Club. This is no ordinary 'Labour Club'. Its commitment to the principles of socialism have been maintained, more or less, throughout its history which goes back to 1896. Dr Johnston was, if not a member, at least a regular visitor to the Club's lectures by people including Keir Hardie, Tom Mann, James Connolly, Ben Tillett, and many of the great figures of British Socialism. The Club was rescued from near-extinction in the early 1980s by an unlikely alliance of Communists, Anarchists and left-wing Labour Party members. It espoused the sort of 'Larger Socialism' which Carpenter advocated. The activists were probably of a similar social composition to the original Bolton Whitman group, in a 20th century context – some teachers, theatre workers, local government employees, union activists. People like Eileen Murphy, Neil Duffield, Wendy and Denis Pye, Jacqueline Dagnall, Shirley Marsland, Don Lee, Gloria Gaffney, Stuart Murray and myself. Carolyn and Rob Masel, and their children were welcome visitors until their return to Australia.

Continuing the tradition

The Whitman Day tradition has continued to this day, with one or two gaps in the late 1980s. The annual celebration takes place on the nearest Saturday to May 31st usually with a moorland stroll by Walker Fold, to Barrow Bridge. It ends at the tea shop by Brian Hey, looking down across Bolton and a scene that was once dominated by hundreds of factory chimneys. The fragility of the original loving cup means it has to stay inside its case, alongside Whitman's canary. A new loving cup is doing its job well and there is

never a lack of people who want to experience what is one of Britain's most unique, and certainly most enjoyable, literary celebrations.

A visit is often made to Wallace's house at 40 Babylon Lane. Until recently the property was owned by Gerry and Janet Thorpe who took a strong interest in the Whitman and Wallace connection, always welcoming visitors.

Other links have been made with American Whitman scholars including Mike Robertson from New Jersey and Joann Krieg from New York; the spiritual connection between Bolton and Whitman has been firmly re-established.

Bolton has recognised that its Whitman links are highly marketable. Several locations around the town now have blue plaques recording their links with the Bolton Whitmanites. One of the founders of the revived Bolton Group, Jacqueline Dagnall, did much of the research and lobbying to make it possible. Many other American academics have been across to work on the archives and perhaps get some spiritual inspiration from walking the moorland paths that Wallace, Johnston and their friends once trod.

The library staff who did so much to help with the original research in 1984 have all retired, but that friendly tradition of assistance has been maintained by today's librarians, many of whom play an active part in the Whitman Day celebrations.

Passing round the Loving Cup - Whitman Day, 2003. Eileen Murphy and Janet Thorpe (left), Janet Thorpe and Jacqueline Dagnall (right). Courtesy ___ an Birthplace Museum

11. CONCLUSION

The original research for this booklet involved issues of sexuality, esoteric philosophy, rival views of Whitman and plenty more. What fun it was! And how many life-long friends have I made as a result. The 'loving comradeship' inspired by Whitman in the mid 1880s is very much alive in Bolton today.

The original group was a most remarkable collection of men and women who succeeded in breaking out of the stuffy moralism of late Victorian society. Through Whitman's poetry they found strength to express a very genuine love for each other in a way that is seldom found today, even within socialist circles.

It was a collective love for each other – not directed at one individual, but shared between several. The success of the group on this level is proved by the remarkably long friendships that were built – from the 1880s to the 1920s and after. The aim of Wallace – to propagate Whitman ideals in the labour movement – was more ambitious. He succeeded for a while: the socialist movement in the 1890s was far more receptive to a semi-mystical, ethical idealism than at any time since. In Wallace's early writings we see this taken to excess, but as he matured he was able to link the need for a socialist society with the Whitmanite themes of love, comradeship, democracy and nature far more effectively.

After the First World War the political space for those sorts of ideas had shrunk. Katherine Glasier was effectively silenced by the parliamentarism of Snowden and Macdonald; and outside the ILP there were few alternatives.

Do they have anything to say to us today? Back in 1984 I gave a qualified 'yes'. Today the response must be even more affirmative, as we risk destroying our planet through greed and thoughtless waste of our natural resources. It's ironic that whilst Marx's view of capitalism falling apart through its own internal contradictions has not happened, climate change – a very direct result of capitalism's untamed forces - is likely to bring about the sort of crisis which Marx foresaw happening through economic collapse.

Since I wrote this in 1984 the world has changed

Plaque unveiled at Bank St. Chapel. Paul Salveson orates, whilst the Mayor looks on amused.

dramatically. The Soviet Union has ceased to exist, ending that experiment for which Wallace and many millions more held out so much hope. China claims to be socialist but it bears little resemblance to anything Wallace would have recognised by the term. The rise of fundamentalism poses obvious threats, but even this is eclipsed by the dangers to the world caused by climate change and degradation of the earth's resources.

The Whitmanites – particularly Wallace, Johnston, and Carpenter – were clear that state socialism on its own wasn't enough and never would meet their desires. They talked of 'The Larger Socialism'. They wanted a society based on love and comradeship, thoroughly democratic, and challenging all the bad old ways of thinking and living. They still have a lot to say to us today.

Whitman remains an inspiring, challenging and annoying figure. I can imagine him having a huge belly laugh at all those academics who try to fit him in to their particular category. Radical socialist poet? Gay icon? Environmentalist? Take your choice, but as soon as you try to categorise and cage this particular bird, he will fly away. Read him, enjoy him, take what is good from him.

SOURCES

Whitman Collection, Bolton Library

Sixsmith and Whiteside Collections,
John Rylands Library

Glasier Collection, Liverpool University Library

Carpenter Collection, Sheffield Library

Feinberg-Whitman Collection, Library of Congess,
Washington

New York Public Library

Monroe Collection, Stanford University Library

Walt Whitman Birthplace Museum papers

Walt Whitman House, Camden NJ

J. Johnston "A Visit to Walt Whitman", 1898

J.Johnston and J.W.Wallace "Visits to Walt Whitman 1890-1", 1917

J. W. Wallace "Walt Whitman and the World Crisis", 1920

Caroline Eccles "A Memoir of J. W. Wallace", 1936

Edward Carpenter "My Days and Dreams", 1916

Edward Carpenter "Days with Walt Whitman", 1906

L. Thompson "The Enthusiasts" (on the Glasiers), 1971

Allen Clarke "Moorlands and Memories", 1985 ed.

Photographs from the Bolton Whitman Collection unless otherwise stated.

Whitman sells tomatoes. A tin can design of the 1950s.

Courtesy Whitman Birthplace Museum